Our School Rules

by Bonita Ferraro

illustrated by Bettina Ogden

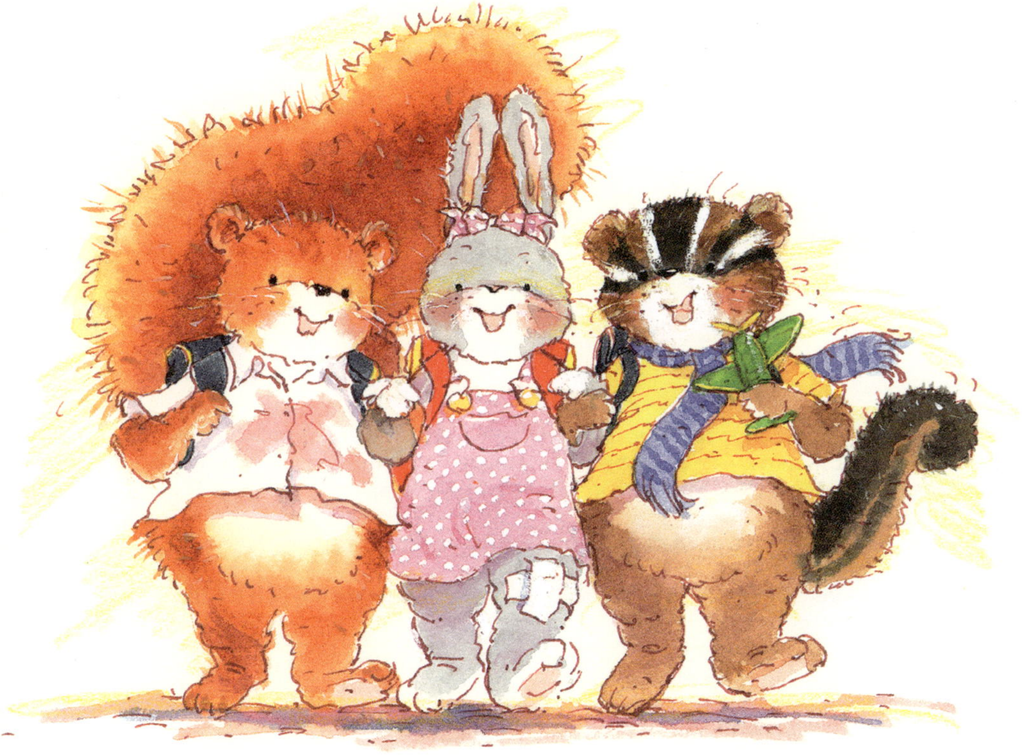

Scott Foresman
is an imprint of

PEARSON

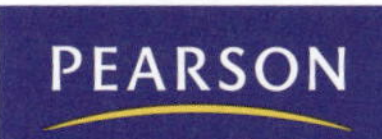

Glenview, Illinois • Boston, Massachusetts • Mesa, Arizona
Shoreview, Minnesota • Upper Saddle River, New Jersey

It was the first day of school for Bunny, Chip, and Scamper.

"We are like a big family. Our household is this school," Mrs. Pine said. "We all have chores to do. We all have rules to follow. Cooperation means working together. Can I count on your cooperation?"

Bunny, Chip, and Scamper
nodded. Mrs. Pine could count on their
cooperation. She could count on them to
be good and to follow the rules.

Later that morning, Bunny was on her way to the playground.

"I am late," Bunny said. "I need to hurry!" Bunny ran down the hall as fast as she could.

"WHOA!" yelled Chip as Bunny
ran into him. Chip's clay plane fell. He
couldn't catch it. It dropped on the floor
and broke.

"I am so sorry, Chip," said Bunny. "I
didn't follow the rule about walking. I
want to be fair. I'll help put your plane
back together."

During recess, Bunny was waiting her turn for the swing. Scamper was next in line.

"When will it be my turn? I want to be next," Scamper said to himself.

Chip got off. Scamper grabbed the swing as hard as he could.

"HEY!" yelled Bunny as she watched Scamper get on the swing. "It is not your turn! It is my turn now!"

"I'm so sorry, Bunny," said Scamper. "I didn't follow the rule about waiting my turn. I want to be fair. I'll let you have your turn."

At lunch, Chip was finished eating first. He was bored. He started to play with his lunch bag.

"I am tired of waiting," Chip said to himself. He blew air into his lunch bag. Then he popped it as loudly as he could.

"YIKES!" yelled Scamper as he jumped in surprise. Scamper's new white shirt had red juice all over it.

"I am so sorry, Scamper," said Chip. "I didn't follow the rule about no noise at lunch. I want to be fair. I'll help you try to wash out the stain."

It was a long first day of school for
the three best friends.

"Tomorrow we should try harder to
follow the rules," said Bunny.

"You can count on us!" her friends
shouted.

Rules, Rules, Rules

Take a look around your school. Do you see any signs that have rules on them? How do you find out about school rules? Are some of the rules in your school the same as the rules in this story?

Every school has rules. In fact, there are rules every place you go. Rules are made to help people stay safe. They also help us to remember to be fair. Think about the rules in your life. How do they keep you safe? How do they help you remember to be fair?